SOUND THE SHOFAR

CLARION BOOKS
TICKNOR & FIELDS: A HOUGHTON MIFFLIN COMPANY
NEW YORK

MIRIAM CHAIKIN

SOUND THE SHOFAR

THE STORY AND MEANING OF ROSH HASHANAH AND YOM KIPPUR

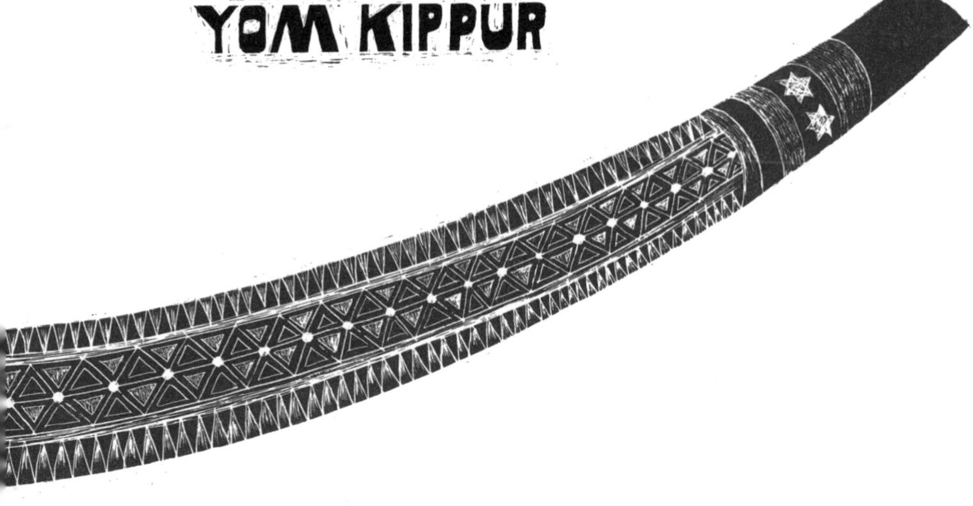

ILLUSTRATED BY ERIKA WEIHS

For the Tikochinsky-Chaikin tree,
and its branches

Acknowledgment
With thanks to Judith Cohen Rosenberg
for reading the book in manuscript form.

Clarion Books
Ticknor & Fields, a Houghton Mifflin Company

Printed in the U.S.A.

v 10 9 8 7 6 5 4 3 2 1

Library of Congress Cataloging-in-Publication Data
Chaikin, Miriam.
Sound the shofar.

Bibliography: p.
Includes index.
Summary: Discusses the origin and development of
Rosh HaShanah and Yom Kippur, their major symbols,
and ways of observing them in the world today and in
different times in history.
1. High Holidays—Juvenile literature.
[1. Rosh HaShanah. 2. Yom Kippur] I. Weihs, Erika,
ill. II. title.
BM693.H5C46 1986 296.4'31 86-2651
ISBN 0-89919-373-0 Paperback ISBN 0-89919-427-3

CONTENTS

BAD
GOOD

DAYS OF AWE

The Jewish holiday of *Rosh HaShanah,* Hebrew for "New Year," starts on the first day of the Hebrew month of *Tishri.* It falls sometime in September or October. Ten days later, *Yom Kippur,* the Day of Atonement, is celebrated. The ten-day period is known as *Yomim Nora'im,* Days of Awe. They are days of awe because people feel fear as well as wonder and reverence. And people are fearful because of the special nature of the holiday — it is a time of judgment.

Holiday Themes

The character of the holiday can be seen in its various themes. The foremost theme is the kingship of God. Most of the holiday is spent in the synagogue, and all prayers and hymns are directed to the greatness of God. God is the king of kings, the greatest power, and the only power.

The creation of the world is another theme, for it is believed that God finished the work of creation on Rosh HaShanah. This day is also known as the birthday of the world.

The idea of judgment pervades the holiday. People are in awe not only because they are being judged by God. They must also judge themselves, asking: Was I honest in my dealings with people? Was I stingy? Was I kind?

Yet another theme is that of forgiveness. Three steps lead to forgiveness: confession, atonement, and repentance. Each depends on the other. Confession is not enough. People must do more. They must atone for their wrongs by asking the people they have wronged for forgiveness. They must also feed the hungry, clothe the naked, and perform other such good deeds. They must also pray to God for forgiveness. But confession and atonement do not count if the third step is not taken. Besides feeling regret, people must promise themselves never to repeat the wrong. They must promise themselves to return to a path of moral goodness.

Symbols and Legends

Libra. Many symbols and legends illustrate the themes and meanings of the holidays. The month of Tishri is Libra on the zodiac. The Libra sign is a balance scale. Jews see the scale as the symbol of judgment. They see deeds being weighed. They say good deeds appear in one dish and bad deeds in the other. If the good deeds outweigh the bad deeds, the person will be forgiven.

Honey. Honey is sweet and has a good taste. It is the very symbol of sweetness and will be found on every table on Rosh HaShanah.

Smelling salts. People must fast on Yom Kippur. Fasting can make a person feel faint. Smelling salts, when inhaled, help revive a person. More commonly seen than store-bought smelling salts is some homemade variety. Often, this is a hearty apple that will last the day. The apple is studded with cloves, a pungent spice. Breathing in the strong fragrance helps revive a person who feels faint because of hunger.

White. The color white is another symbol of the holidays. White stands for purity. Many people wear white on Yom Kippur. The synagogue is draped in white. A white curtain hangs over the Holy Ark where the *Torah* is kept. The Torah itself, the Bible in scroll form, is also draped in white.

The Heavenly Court. Human beings are limited in knowledge. Even the most brilliant of us can know only so much. We are also limited in how long we live. All of us will die one day. We are limited in other ways as well. God is very different. God is all-knowing and eternal. God existed before the world began and will exist if the world should ever disappear.

This idea is hard for mortals to grasp. How does a power that we cannot see pass judgment on us? Where does a power that is eternal live? The ancient rabbis looked for ways to make God more understandable to the people. So they began to speak of God as a king and as a judge, two mighty figures whom the people knew firsthand. They said that God convened a heavenly court on Rosh HaShanah. And the story of the heavenly court has come to be the most popular legend of the holidays and one that well explains their meanings.

At the heavenly court were angels dressed in white. Two of them acted as lawyers. Sanegor was a good angel. He defended the people. Kategor, the evil angel, accused the people. Kategor was *HaSatan,* Satan.

Open before God were three books: the Book of Life, the Book of Death, and the Book of Judgment. The names of saintly people who had been chosen to live another year had already been entered in the Book of Life. Wicked people were scheduled to die and their names had been entered in the Book of Death. Everyone else is listed in the third book, the Book of Judgment. Throughout the ten-day period, the Days of Awe, each person's name comes up for review. Sanegor ar-

gues that the name should be entered in the Book of Life. Kategor wants it entered in the Book of Death.

No one need really worry. Kategor has never been known to win a case. Besides, the books stay open for all ten days. They are sealed only on Yom Kippur, when the final judgment is made. People have a chance to change their fate if they have misbehaved. Anyone who confesses, atones, and repents during the Days of Awe can expect to be inscribed in the Book of Life.

While Kategor — Satan — has never won in the heavenly court, he has been known to force his will on earth. He is the symbol of evil. And evil has snuffed out the lives of many people whose names had been entered in the Book of Life.

The rabbis try to explain evil by saying that God created a wonderful world and that it is up to the people themselves to find a way to end evil.

The idea for the Book of Life comes from two episodes in Jewish history. The first concerns Moses and the Ten Commandments. When he came down from the mountain with the Ten Commandments written on two tablets, Moses found the Israelites worshiping a golden calf that they had made. In anger, he broke the tablets. Then he went back up the mountain to plead with God to forgive the people. He said, *Oh, this people have sinned a great sin, and have made them a god of gold. Even so, if You will, forgive their sin. And if not, blot me, I pray you, out of Your book.* God answered, *Whoever has sinned against Me, him will I blot out of My book.*

The second episode where a book of the living is discussed appears later in history, in the time of Ezra, around 586 B.C.E. The Babylonians destroyed the Jewish Temple in Jerusalem, took the Jews captive, and sent them to Babylon. Fifty years later, a kinder conqueror told them to go back to Jerusalem. There, the names of the known Jews were entered in a book to keep track of the Jewish nation.

Shofar, or ram's horn. The *shofar* is the main symbol of the holiday. It is blown on Rosh HaShanah to announce the start of a new year, and on Yom Kippur to end the Days of Awe and the Yom Kippur fast. The horn has been a symbol of the Jews throughout biblical history. In the Bible story about Abraham and his son Isaac, we read that God tells Abraham to sacrifice his son and that Abraham prepares to do so. But a ram appears and is sacrificed instead. The ram's horn is a symbol of rescue. It is also a symbol of faith, as demonstrated by Abraham's willingness to obey God.

The horn blasts are themselves echoes of ancient history. The Bible tells us that the Israelites of Moses' day, when they stood at the foot of Mount Sinai, experienced the presence of God amid thunder, lightning, columns of smoke, and blasts of horns

At other times, when Moses wished to assemble the people in the Israelite camp, nine long blasts were blown on the horn. Nine short blasts were the signal for people to take down their tents and break camp. The priests left the camp first, carrying the Ark that held the tablets. The next nine long blasts were the signal for the people to follow the priests out of the camp.

The horn remained a major symbol in the life of the Jewish people. It was sounded at every important occasion — to call soldiers together, to signal the start of a festival, to announce the beginning of the reign of a new king, and to let the people know that the king had entered the town and was about to appear.

A popular legend has grown up around the historic and dramatic events announced by shofar blasts. Jews have been waiting for the arrival of the Messiah for some two thousand years. They wait for him — or it, if the

Messiah is an event — because the coming of the Messiah is supposed to bring an end to war, hatred, and poverty and launch a new era of love and harmony between all people. The shofar is blown on Rosh HaShanah, according to the story, to upset Satan. Why? His evil doings are over. Or so he believes. For when he hears the blasts, he thinks it is because the Messiah has arrived. Now he must disappear from history.

Other Names of the Holiday

The High Holy Days is another name for Rosh HaShanah and Yom Kippur. The ten-day period is also called *Aseret Yemay Teshuvah* — the Ten Days of Repentance.

Other names for Rosh HaShanah:

Yom HaDin — Day of Judgment
Yom Teruah — Day of Shofar Blowing
Yom Zicharon — Day of Remembrance (God remembers us, we remember God, and we also remember our loved ones who have died)

In ancient times Yom Kippur was called Trumpet Feast. It is also known as *Tzomah Rabbah* — the Great Fast, and *Tzom Lavan*, the White Fast.

Laws for celebrating holidays and laws for the duties of priests appear in the Bible book called Leviticus. Ancient Hebrew priests were called Levites because they were chosen from the tribe of Levi. *Leviticus* is Latin for "priests."

HOW THE HOLIDAYS DEVELOPED

The holiday of Rosh HaShanah has its early origin around 1700 B.C.E., in the time of Abraham and Sarah. Months did not yet have names but were referred to by their position in the year — first month, second, third, and so on.

Abraham and Sarah left their home in Ur (Iraq today) with their clan and headed for Canaan. At that time, people worshiped many gods. And God told Abraham to go to Canaan and found there a new nation, one that worshiped only God. Abraham and Sarah were the first people to worship God alone, and the first Jews, then called Hebrews. God promised them the land of Canaan for their descendants.

As Abraham and Sarah and their clan journeyed through the desert on the way to the Promised Land, they marveled over God's wonders. The sky showed great order. The moon began as a sliver one night, grew to be round over succeeding nights, then became a sliver again. The pattern was unchanging. This great order was seen as the work of God, of the Almighty. And to pay tribute to God, Abraham and Sarah and their clan celebrated the arrival of each new moon. One in the group, the trumpeter, blew short blasts on the ram's horn to signal the start of another new cycle of the moon. Then the people sat down together to feast and make merry. They celebrated *Rosh Chodesh,* the start of a new month, which came to be known as the New Moon Festival.

In Canaan, Abraham and Sarah and their children and their children's children continued to celebrate Rosh Chodesh. In time, the New Moon celebration of the seventh month became more important than all others. The reason is not known. But the appearance of the new moon in the seventh month was greeted with much horn blowing — long and loud blasts. The New Moon Festival of the seventh month would disappear in time and Rosh HaShanah, New Year, would take its place.

Joseph

Joseph in the Bible was the great-grandson of Abraham and Sarah. An episode in the Joseph story was the basis of a custom that later became part of the New Year celebration.

Joseph's brothers were jealous of Joseph because he was the favorite of their father, Jacob. One day, the brothers threw Joseph into a dry well and left him to die. To remove blame from themselves, they "set up" a murder. They killed a goat, smeared Joseph's coat with its blood, and showed the bloodstained coat to their father, to make it appear that Joseph had been killed by a wild animal.

The goat had been killed to provide the brothers with a way to cover up their sin. It was made to take the blame and pay the price. In years to come, this idea would be formalized in a special ceremony of the New Year celebration in Jerusalem. The idea of transferring sin to another has entered the English language through the word *scapegoat,* an innocent person who is falsely accused or made to take the blame for the misdeeds of another.

Moses

Joseph did not die in the dry well. He was rescued and went on to be appointed governor of Egypt by the Pharaoh. In later history, the Jews were enslaved by another Pharaoh. Moses, the great prophet and leader, freed them, took them out of Egypt, and led them back to Canaan. On the way, he formed them into a God-worshiping nation.

Moses taught the Jews the moral laws that God wanted them to live by. He organized their religion by building the first shrine to God, a tent that held the tablets with the Ten Commandments, and by naming his brother Aaron as high priest. Moses kept the nation together by seeing to it that the people obeyed God's laws and kept their festivals, including the New Moon Festival in the seventh month. He taught the people the idea of atonement, and how to atone for their sins.

In Canaan

When the Jews settled in Canaan they became farmers. They continued to celebrate Passover, which was their Exodus-from-Egypt freedom holiday. They also celebrated the New Year festival of the seventh month. As farmers, they were dependent on their crops. There were now new occasions to celebrate. In early summer, when the first wheat was cut, they celebrated Shavuot, the Festival of Weeks. In the fall, when fruits and grapes were gathered, they celebrated Sukkot, the Festival of Booths. This holiday, which they celebrated on the fifteenth day of the seventh month, became their greatest festival. In time, Sukkot would lead to the creation of Yom Kippur, the Day of Atonement.

The First Temple

Around 955 B.C.E., King Solomon, son of King David, built a magnificent Temple in Jerusalem to replace the tent the Jews had built in the desert. The tablets of the Law were transferred to the new Temple.

Jerusalem, always crowded, was thick with people in the seventh month. It was the scene of almost continuous celebration. The Festival of the New Moon took place on the first day of the month. Then people began preparing for Sukkot, which started on the fifteenth. Because thousands of pilgrims were in Jerusalem then, King Solomon chose the seventh month to dedicate the Temple to God. The custom of wearing white on Yom Kippur took shape in the early days of the Temple. The high priest wore white, a symbol of purity. Solomon, in urging his people to be pure, said, "Let your garments always be white." And the form of atonement that Moses had taught was practiced. If people wished to atone for a wrong they had committed, they brought a goat to the Temple. It was sacrificed on the altar, in one of the many ceremonies of the day, as a sin offering.

Babylon

Meanwhile, in countries bordering Canaan, new empires arose. Their kings, in search of more territory and treasure, made war on the Jews. In 586 B.C.E., Babylonia (Iraq today) conquered Jerusalem and destroyed Solomon's Temple. In the style of the time, the Babylonian king separated the Jewish leaders — the king, nobles, teachers, priests, and their families — from their land. He took them captive and brought them to Babylon, his great capital, over five hundred miles away. The rest of the Jewish people were left in their homeland.

New Ideas

In Babylon, the Jews clung to their beliefs and customs. They no longer had a Temple at which to offer sacrifices. But they set up schools and built synagogues, to preserve their way of life. And they kept their festivals. They also borrowed some ideas from the Babylonians.

The Babylonians had names for their months. And the Jews named their own months. They called the seventh month Tishri. The Babylonians celebrated a Day of Judgment at which their various gods assembled to judge them and to write the fate of each person on a tablet. The Jewish idea for the Book of Life began to take shape here. Jewish sages now spoke in poetic terms about God, saying God reigned like a king in a heavenly court, surrounded by angels dressed in white robes.

In the absence of the pageantry at the Temple, Jews found a greater spiritual meaning in the quieter celebration of Rosh Chodesh, the New Moon Festival. Gradually, the moon aspect began to fade from the celebration. Now the Jewish sages associated the first day of Tishri with God's creation of the world. They called the day *Yom Harat Olam,* the Day the World Was Created.

Second Temple

Fifty years later, Cyrus the Great of Persia (Iran today) defeated Babylonia. Cyrus helped the Jews return to their land and urged them to rebuild their Temple. The Temple that was rebuilt was less grand than the first.

The Jews who returned to Jerusalem were surprised at the condition of the Jews who had remained behind. In fifty years, the Jerusalem Jews had fallen out of touch with their roots. Living without scholars and teachers, they had forgotten their laws and holidays.

In 444 B.C.E., Nehemiah and Ezra called a meeting of the Jews on the first day of the seventh month.

Nehemiah was the Jewish governor of Jerusalem. Ezra was a descendant of Aaron, the first high priest. They met in front of the Water Gate of the Temple. Ezra and Nehemiah, with other leaders, stood on a platform. And Ezra read aloud the laws of Moses. Ashamed of how much they had forgotten, the people began to cry. Nehemiah comforted them, saying, *Go your way, eat the fat, and drink the sweet, and send portions unto those who have less than you, for this day is holy to God.*

That day in front of the Water Gate was the first celebration of Rosh HaShanah, although the holiday was not yet so named.

The Temple again became the center for celebration. And the 15th of Tishri, Sukkot, was a time of drinking, feasting, dance, and song. But the sages who had returned from Babylon were distressed by the sight of such revelry. Where were thoughts of God in all the merry-making?

To balance the merrymaking, they introduced a somber note earlier in the month of Tishri. They declared the tenth day to be the start of the new year and a day of atonement. The merrymaking was slowed down, up to a point. In the morning, people atoned for their sins by bringing lambs and goats to offer up as sin offerings. In the afternoon, they feasted, drank wine, and had a good time. It became a time for young people to find husbands and wives. Maidens dressed in white danced in the vineyards and sang to the young men standing about:

> Young man, lift up your eyes, whom will you choose?
> Do not look for beauty, look for a good family,
> For fortune is deceitful and beauty is vain,
> But a woman who fears the Lord is to be praised.

The sages acted again. This time they created two separate holidays, on two separate days. They declared the tenth day to be Yom Kippur, a day of atonement. And the first day of the month, the time when the New Moon Festival used to be celebrated, they made the start of the new year — Rosh HaShanah.

Herod Beautifies the Temple

In Canaan, now called Judea, wars and conquests continued to bring changes for the Jews. They were ruled by, among others, Greece, Egypt, and finally Rome. In 37 B.C.E., Rome appointed Herod, a wealthy man, king of the Jews. To win favor with Rome, Herod built cities and named them after the Roman emperor. To win favor with the Jews, he rebuilt the Temple with marble and gold and made it into one of the marvels of the age. Chariots clattered in and out of its many gates. Nicanor's Gate, so named for the man who paid for it, was huge. Two hundred men were needed to open and shut it. Besides the main rooms of the Temple, there were many smaller rooms off its various halls. The Sanhedrin, the Jewish supreme court, met in one such room.

HOW THE HOLIDAYS WERE CELEBRATED IN ANCIENT JERUSALEM

In the last days of the Temple, the holiday period was a time of almost continuous activity. Shofar blasts coming from the Temple announced the arrival of the new moon, beginning the new month and the new year. It was the start of Rosh HaShanah. Did the people living in other cities of Judea — in Safed, Tiberias, Hebron, and elsewhere — hear the blasts from Jerusalem? They did not. Jerusalem was too far away. They were notified of the start of a holiday by smoke signals.

In Jerusalem, before the horns were blown, witnesses watched the sky. There were no firm calendars or clocks then. When the people saw the new moon, they ran to tell the Sanhedrin, at the Temple. The Sanhedrin gave the signal for trumpets to be blown and for fires to be lit on hilltops. Everyone saw and heard the signals all over the land. And within moments, everyone began the celebration at the same time.

Yom Kippur

On Yom Kippur, the people fasted. Though they denied themselves the pleasure of food, they called the holiday "Trumpets Feast." They used the word "feast" playfully and poetically. They stopped eating when they heard the trumpets and instead feasted on thoughts of God.

The ceremonies at the Temple were many and lasted all day. People dressed in white. It was the custom to ask friends and relatives for forgiveness. Everyone gathered in the Temple courtyard for three public confessions.

The First Confession. The high priest, dressed in white, represented the people before God. The first confession was for himself and his family. A bull that would be sacrificed was brought before him. Placing his hands on the head of the bull, he spoke the words of the first confession: *I beseech Thee, O Lord, I have sinned, I have been iniquitous, I have transgressed against Thee, I and my*

household. I beseech Thee, O Lord, pardon the sins and iniquities and transgressions which I have committed against Thee, I and my household.

On this one day a year, the people prostrated themselves in answer. They lowered themselves to the ground and said, *Blessed be the Name, Whose glorious kingdom is forever and ever.*

What did they mean by "the Name"? Today people freely say "God" and "Jehovah." In ancient times the words were regarded as too holy to utter. Instead, people said "Lord," "*Adonai*," "*Elohim*," or "the Name." In Hebrew, the sacred name of God is spelled Yud(י), Hay(ה), Vav(ו), Hay(ה). It could be spoken only by the high priest and only on Yom Kippur. The letters, moved about, spell the three Hebrew words for "is," "was," and "will be." They express the majesty and eternity of God. The Hebrew letters transliterated into English became *YHWH.* When vowels were added, this became Yahweh or Jahweh, and also, less correctly, Jehovah.

The Second Confession. Two goats were then brought before the high priest. From an urn he withdrew two gold disks, one marked "For YHWH," the other "For Azazel." *Azazel* was an evil spirit that lived in the wilderness. The high priest placed a label on the head of each goat. The goat that received the "For YHWH" disk was to be sacrificed to God. Over this goat he cried, *A sin offering for YHWH.*

Blessed be the Name, Whose glorious kingdom is forever and ever, the people answered.

The people of that day, like some people today, believed that sins could be transferred to someone or something else. In a ceremony soon to follow, the high priest would transfer the sins of the people to the second goat. Meanwhile, he tied a red sash — red because that color was believed to frighten away other evil spirits — around the horn of the scapegoat. Then he turned back to the bull. Repeating the same words, he made a second confession, this time for the priests. The people again prostrated themselves, and answered with the same words.

The Holy of Holies. Then came the tensest moment of the day. The Holy of Holies was the most sacred room in the Temple. No one was allowed inside. It contained the Holy Ark, which held the Torah. The spirit of God was believed to dwell in that room. On this one day in the year the high priest was allowed to enter. Before he did so, he was escorted to the Temple in an impressive parade.

This description of the parade is attributed to Marcus, a Roman consul, in Jerusalem:

> And this have I seen with my own eyes: First to go before the high priest would be all those who were of the seed of the kings of Israel; after them went all those who were descended from the kings of the house of David. A herald would go before them crying, "Give honor to the house of David!" After them came the house of Levi, and a herald crying, "Give honor to the house of Levi!" All the prefects wore clothing of blue silk, and the priests, of whom there were

> 24,000, white silk. After them came the singers and musicians. Then came the seventy of the Sanhedrin and after them a hundred priests with a silver rod in their hands, to clear the way, and after them the high priest, then the priests. And the heads of academies stood up and cried, "Lord High Priest, may you come in peace! Pray to our Maker to grant us long life, that we may engage in His Torah."

On this day, and only on this day, the high priest called God by name, YHWH. And inside he prayed to God and asked forgiveness for all the people.

The Third Confession — the Scapegoat. The high priest emerged from the Holy of Holies cleansed and radiant. Relieved to have the awesome moments over, the high priest and the people now turned their attention to the "Azazel" goat. Placing his hands on the head of the goat, the high priest repeated the confession for a third time, now for all the people. As he finished, he looked at the people and said, *Ye shall be clean.* And for the last time that day, the people prostrated themselves and again answered, *Blessed be the Name, Whose glorious kingdom is forever and ever.*

Now the priests whose job it was to lead the Azazel goat into the wilderness did so. Laden with the sins of the people, the scapegoat departed from Jerusalem and disappeared. The fear arose that a scapegoat might come wandering back to Jerusalem with all the sins. To keep this from happening, the priests decided to lead the goat to the edge of a cliff and push it over. The goat died and so did not return.

Neilat Shearim — The Closing of the Gates. Yom Kippur was over. Before the Temple gates were closed, the high priest blessed the people. He parted the fingers of each hand, three on one side, two on the other. Then, thumbs touching, arms upraised, he said, *May God bless you and take care of you. May God cause His countenance to shine upon you. May God turn His face unto you and bring you peace.*

Everyone left the Temple in a good mood. Many tried to reach the high priest, to kiss his hand. At home, people ate food and broke their fasts. Then they went out to their yard or rooftop and put up a few boards. Already, they had begun to build a *sukkah* — a booth for the holiday of Sukkot, which was four days away.

CUSTOMS ADDED IN EXILE

Rome was at first a tolerant ruler in Judea, and Jews were able to worship as they pleased. Jews mourned the assassination of Julius Caesar in 44 B.C.E. In time, however, Roman rulers became cruel and corrupt. Some believed themselves to be divine and insisted on being worshiped.

Jews are forbidden by their religion to worship anyone but God. They rebelled against the Romans, and a long war broke out. In 70 C.E., Roman soldiers set fire to the Temple, destroyed Jerusalem, and forbade Jews ever to return. To erase the connection between the land and the Jews, Rome changed the name of Jerusalem to Aeolina Capitalina and of Judea to Palestine.

The destruction of Jerusalem and the Temple did not end Jewish civilization. The Jews were tied to a belief in God. They were linked as much to a way of life as to a land. The brilliant ancient civilizations of Greece and Rome are gone, but the Jews remain. They settled in other cities in Palestine and in all the known lands of the world, taking their religion and their customs with them.

The dispersion created three distinct groups of Jews. In the third century C.E., Christianity became a world religion, and Jews lived in Christian lands. In the sixth century, Islam, the Muslim faith, arose, and Jews lived in Muslim lands. The group that lived in Muslim lands spoke Arabic and came to be called Oriental Jews. The group that lived in Spain and spoke Spanish were known as *Sephardim.* The Hebrew word for Spain is *Sepharad.* The third group lived in and around Germany. "Germany" in Hebrew is *Ashkenaz.* German-speaking Jews are called *Ashkenazim.*

In recent times a fourth and much smaller group of Jews was discovered. Living in Ethiopia, and cut off from other Jewish communities for some two thousand years, were black Jews. They observed the Jewish rit-

uals and laws. Other Ethiopians called them Falasha, which in their language means "stranger." But the black Jews call themselves Beta Israel — the House of Israel.

Their origins are not known. Some say they are the descendants of the son born to the Queen of Sheba and King Solomon. Others say they are descended from the tribe of Dan, one of the original twelve tribes of Israel. There are still other claims. Whatever their origin, the Beta Israel have remained faithful to Jewish tradition, often in the face of great danger.

In 1985, after two thousand years, they were united with their people. In a dramatic move, the government of Israel flew some ten thousand Ethiopian Jews to the land of Israel.

The Jews, scattered to the four corners of the earth, held fast to their beliefs and celebrated their holidays. But their ceremonies changed. The Temple in Jerusalem that had been the center of worship for a thousand years was gone. Gone also was the altar of sacrifice. The priests had no duties. In the diaspora — a Greek word meaning dispersion or scattering — everything started to change. Life in exile began to shape a new system of worship.

Rabbis — teachers — began to take the place of priests. Instead of a central temple, individual synagogues began to spring up in Jewish communities all over the world. Instead of relying on a high priest to be an intermediary for the people to God, rabbis encouraged the people to become like the high priest themselves, to lead moral lives, to be pure, and to pray to God directly, on their own.

Viddui — Confession

In the third century C.E., the main rabbis were in Babylonia. They tried to unify holiday customs, so Jews all over the world would celebrate in the same way. In olden days, the high priest used to confess by saying, *I have sinned, I have committed iniquity, I have transgressed.* The rabbis decided those words were too general and that more specific language was needed. They said each individual was responsible for his or her acts. Each individual had to confess for himself or herself.

The rabbis took the view that no one is free of sin. They composed two sets of confessions for everyone to recite aloud and together. One is called the Shorter Confession and begins, *We have sinned, we have been unfaithful, we have cheated, and stolen, we have spoken unfairly.*

The Longer Confession in Hebrew is alphabetical. In those days, the printing press had not yet been invented. Books were written by hand and were scarce. Alphabetical order was an aid to memorization. In English the confession begins, *Forgive us, O God our Father, for the sin which we have sinned before You by selfishness.* Many sins are mentioned. The same opening words precede each sin: *Forgive us, O God our Father, for the sin which we have sinned before You by thoughtlessness. Forgive us, O God our Father, for the sin which we have sinned before You by deceit. Forgive us, O God our Father, for the sin which we have sinned before You by wronging our friends* — and so on, including "wicked thoughts," "disobeying parents and teachers," and other wrongs.

Kol Nidre — All Vows

Jewish prayers take their names from the opening words of the prayer. *Kol Nidre,* "All Vows," are the opening words of a statement chanted before Yom Kippur services begin. Although the rabbis of every age have tried to suppress Kol Nidre, this ceremony has come to be the very symbol of Yom Kippur.

Ancient people used to vow. (And the practice still exists in modern life.) To give weight to a promise, they used to say, "I swear before God." To God they used to say, "Please help me and I will never again do thus-and-so."

The rabbis greatly opposed the habit of vowing. They quoted the Torah: *When you make a vow to God, do not put off fulfilling it, for God will require it of you, and you will have incurred guilt; whereas you incur no guilt if you refrain from vowing.* They told people it was morally wrong to make a vow and not keep it. And that it was against the Law if the vow involved God's name. For the Third Commandment says, *You shall not take the name of God in vain.*

All the rabbis' efforts came to naught. People vowed, then were unhappy when they could not fulfill a vow. Some even spoke of killing themselves. The rabbis had to do something. Vowing had consequences. Vowing led to problems. Since they could not stop the vowing, they tried to control it.

To deal with a broken vow, they introduced the idea of a court. It met on Rosh HaShanah. Three learned men acted as judges. They were empowered to excuse a vow if circumstances merited it. Their authority,

כל־נדרי ואסרי
וחרמי וקונמי וכנויי
וקנוסי ושבועות
דנדרנא ודאשתבענא
ודאחרימנא ודאסרנא
על נפשתנא מיום
כפורים
זה
עד
יום....

however, was limited. They could judge only vows made in the name of God or to God. All other vows were outside their jurisdiction. A vow against a person could be excused or forgiven only by that person. Under no circumstance could a vow made in a court of law be excused.

The rabbis created a formula for people who could not stop themselves from vowing. The formula was said publicly on Rosh HaShanah: *Every vow (Kol Nidre) which I may make in the future shall be null.*

Over the centuries, rabbis continued to oppose this practice. But the people continued to excuse themselves with the Kol Nidre statement. Some used the future tense, as above. Some used the past tense: *Every vow which I have made in the past year shall be null.*

The weakness of human flesh and events of Jewish history kept the Kol Nidre alive over the protests of the rabbis.

In the seventh century C.E., Spain was overrun by a barbarian people, the Visigoths. They tortured and persecuted Jews and forced them to renounce their religion. To save their lives, many Jews publicly renounced their faith, but practiced their religion in secret. The public act pained them. They received comfort by canceling the vows in their own minds through repeating the words of Kol Nidre in the synagogue.

In the thirteenth century, the Jews of Spain again found comfort in the Kol Nidre statement. The new Christian king and queen tried to force the Jews to convert. The method used was a decree that said only Christians could hold good jobs. To save their livelihoods, many Jews converted publicly but practiced their religion in secret. Spanish Christians called them Marranos, which means "swine."

By now, the Kol Nidre chant had shifted to Yom Kippur, probably because more people attended the synagogue services on that day.

The secret Jews, as the Marranos were also called, went to the Christian church secretly but practiced their Jewish customs at home. They thought of themselves as sinners. And so were they viewed by the rabbis and by other Jews who did not undergo conversion. The presence in the synagogue on Yom Kippur of the secret Jews created a new ritual. Before the Kol Nidre was chanted, the rabbi declared aloud, *By authority of the court on high, and by authority of the court on earth, with the knowledge of the Almighty, and with the knowledge of the congregation, we declare it lawful to pray in the company of sinners.*

In 1492 all Jews were forcibly expelled from Spain. Many fled to Portugal, where they enjoyed a degree of freedom for a while. Portuguese Jews were later also faced with forced conversion. They, too, became secret Jews who found comfort in saying the words of the Kol Nidre.

Kapparot — Atonements and Substitutions

Kapparot comes from the same word as *(Yom) Kippur* and means "atonements." It has also come to mean "substitutions."

The idea of transferring sins, even symbolically, appealed to people. It allowed them to feel clean and pure again. The scapegoat disappeared from Yom Kippur, but versions of the ceremony remained after the exile and still remain today.

The ancient Jews of Babylonia transferred their sins to the chicken or fish they would eat for dinner that night. Since the creature was due to lose its life in any event, they performed a "substitution" ceremony. They twirled the chicken or fish over their own heads, and the head of each child, three times. And they transferred their sins to it, saying, *This is my (your) substitute, this is my (your) exchange, this is my (your) atonement. This fowl (fish) will go to death and I (you) will enter upon a good, long and peaceful life.* Or they might have said, *If I deserve punishment for my sins, let this creature be a substitute for me.*

Adults found the ceremony comforting, and for children it was a lot of fun.

Rabbis tried to banish this custom too. They called it a foolish superstition. Since they could not stop the people from performing Kapparot, they tried to at least turn it into a good deed. They created a custom of donating the fowl or fish to a poor family of the town, or to give the equivalent of what the meal cost to charity.

Tashlich — Casting Away

Tashlich, which means "cast away," is another ceremony that grew out of the scapegoat idea.

Besides creating the Kapparot ceremony for Yom Kippur, the ancient Jews of Babylonia created yet another ceremony for Rosh HaShanah. The people were superstitious. They believed evil spirits lived in water, the way the earlier Jews of Jerusalem believed evil spirits lived in the wilderness. They tried to pacify the evil spirits. They planted peas and beans in baskets, then cast the baskets into the river, to feed the evil spirits.

The rabbis tried to abolish this custom too. Not only did they not succeed, but the custom spread to Europe, where people believed their sins clung to their garments in the form of evil spirits. On Rosh HaShanah, they went to a river or some other body of water. They turned their pockets inside out and shook their garments out over the water. Relieved, they watched the current carry away their sins.

The rabbis of Europe banned this custom as well, but people would not give it up. Since the rabbis could not stop the practice, they sought to rid the custom of the superstition. They tried to banish the element of evil spirits. They told the people to put bread crumbs in their pockets, or handkerchiefs, and to regard the bread crumbs as symbolic sins. The idea took hold. The evil spirits disappeared, and a bread crumb ceremony has come down to our own times in that form.

Today, the Tashlich ceremony is also associated with the prophet Micah. He lived and preached in Jerusalem in the eighth century B.C.E., before Greece arose as a world power. Many people of his day, like many people today, were selfish and greedy. Like all prophets, he preached to the people to obey God's moral laws. He told them God wanted three things of them: that they act justly, love mercy, and walk humbly with God. If they left the path of evil and returned to the path of good, he promised that God would forgive them and would "cast their sins into the depths of the sea."

Unetanneh Tokef Kedushat HaYom — Let Us Proclaim the Holiness of this Day

Unetanneh tokef kedushat HaYom are the opening words of a prayer said on Rosh HaShanah. The prayer is also a memorial to Rabbi Amnon of Mainz, who lived in Germany in the eleventh century C.E. According to a legend, Rabbi Amnon was given a choice by the authorities: to convert to Christianity or die. The rabbi refused to convert. He was punished by having his hands and feet cut off. On Rosh HaShanah, Rabbi Amnon was carried on a litter to the synagogue. As his lips spoke the last words of the Unetanneh Tokef, he died. It is the only prayer in the prayer book dedicated to the memory of an individual. The words appear later in this book, in the chapter titled "Rosh HaShanah."

כסלו
חשון
תשרי
אלול
אב
תמוז
סיון
אייר
ניסן
אדר
שבט
טבת

THE JEWISH CALENDAR FOR THE DAYS OF AWE

Elul (August–September)	Adar (February–March)
Tishri (September–October)	Nisan (March–April)
Heshvan (October–November)	Iyar (April–May)
Kislev (November–December)	Sivan (May–June)
Tevet (December–January)	Tammuz (June–July)
Shevat (January–February)	Av (July–August)

The Jewish calendar has twelve months. An extra month is added in a leap year.

A year is a cycle of time. Each individual has a personal year that begins on his or her birth date. The new school year begins in September. The business year begins in yet another month. So, too, the Jewish calendar contains various years.

The month of Shevat starts the year of trees.

Nisan starts the year of history of the Jewish nation. The ancient Jews were slaves in Egypt. They became free in the month of Nisan. In that month, they marched out of Egypt and on to Canaan, the Promised Land, a free nation.

Tishri marks a new year in the religious life of the individual person. It is very special and calls for special blessings, prayers, greetings, and customs. It is so special that Jews begin preparing for the new religious year in the month before, the month of Elul. This is why Elul has been placed at the head of the calendar.

HOW THE HOLIDAYS ARE CELEBRATED TODAY

There is not one kind of Jew but many kinds. Religious Jews vary from liberal to orthodox, with many shades in between. Jews also differ culturally. They live in all parts of the world and in many lands. This may account for a difference in custom. But, while ceremonies may vary from place to place, the basic celebration of the holidays at home and in the synagogue is the same the world over.

Elul — Getting in the Mood

In Elul, people begin preparing for the holidays. The word *Elul* is an acrostic formed from the first letters of each word of a phrase spoken by King Solomon: *Ani l'dodi udodi li* — "I am my beloved's and my beloved is mine." The beloved is God. And in Elul people begin to turn their thoughts away from business, school, and other concerns. They turn instead toward more spiritual matters, toward holiness and thoughts of God.

To prepare for the holidays, people need not buy or equip themselves with anything in particular. It is themselves they must prepare. The month of Tishri will soon be upon them. And they will be spending a great deal of time in the synagogue, at prayer. They will be in the "presence of God," as it were. So they must purify their thoughts and put themselves in the right frame of mind for such an awesome experience.

Besides "being in the presence of God," they will also be judged on Rosh HaShanah. The heavenly books are being prepared now, in Elul. Everyone's name is being inscribed in one of the books.

But there are many people in the world. How do the angels in heaven keep track of who did what over the year? A popular folk tale offers one answer: Each person has a book in heaven. Each night, while the body sleeps, the soul rises up and records the day's doings. The angels read each book and, according to the record, transfer the name of the person to the Book of Life, the Book of Death, or the Book of Judgment.

In Elul people also begin judging themselves, to put themselves in the right mood for the holiday. *Whom have I hurt?* they ask. *Where have I done harm?* They draw closer to family and friends. They link themselves to past generations by visiting the graves of relatives and loved ones.

The Jews of India prepare themselves for the long Yom Kippur fast by eating only one meal a day during Elul. They cleanse themselves spiritually by praying daily. On the last day of Elul, men divide themselves into two

groups at the synagogue. One group rises and recites a prayer of forgiveness, whereupon the other says, *As we forgive you, so may you be forgiven on high.* The second group then rises and repeats the same procedure. Then the men perform a hand kiss, *Haath boshi* in the Marathi Indian dialect. Each person presses the hand of his neighbor between his own two hands. Then he transfers the hand kiss to himself by touching his own fingertips to his lips. Men and boys go home to kiss the hand of their mothers and sisters.

In the synagogue, the shofar is sounded each morning. Throughout the month, special prayers called *Selichot* — "forgiveness" — are said. Sephardim say Selichot daily. Ashkenazim begin saying them on the last Saturday night before Rosh HaShanah.

"לשנה טובה
תכתבו ותחתמו"

GREETINGS, BLESSINGS AND PSALMS

Greetings

Already in Elul, people begin exchanging New Year greetings. They write and phone to wish each other a healthy, happy, and sweet new year. They exchange printed cards. The most popular greetings are le-sha-NA tow-VA tik-a-TAY-vu ve-te-KHA-TAY-mu, "May you be inscribed (in the Book of Life) and sealed for a good year," and sha-NA tow-VA u-me-tu-KA, "May the year be good and sweet." All other greetings are variations of these, including the most commonly heard, simply le-sha-NA tow-VA, "For a good year."

Blessings

The riches of the world are many and varied. They are not to be taken for granted. To assure that they are not, a blessing is said over each and every thing.

For the new moon:
Ye-HI ra-TZON mi-le-fa-NE-kha
A-dow-NAI E-lo-HAY-nu v'El-o-HAY a-vo-TAY-nu
Sheh-te-kha-DESH a-LAY-nu et ha-KHO-desh ha-ZEH
Le-tow-VAH u-le-ve-ra-HAH.

May it be Your will, O God
And God of our fathers,
To renew us this month
For goodness and blessing.

When lighting candles:
Ba-RUKH a-TA a-dow-NAI El-o-HAY-nu ME-lekh ha-o-LAM,
a-SHER kid-e-SHA-nu b'mitz-vo-TAV v'tzi-VA-nu
le-had-LIK nair shel yom-TOV.

Praised be God, King of the universe,
Who blessed us with good teachings and
Commanded us to light holiday candles.

All blessings of food begin with the same words: *ba-RUKH a-TA A-dow-NAI El-o-HAY-nu Me-LEKH ha-o-LAM,* Praised be God, King of the universe. Only the next sentence changes, according to the food.

Wine: bo-RAY pri ha-GA-fen, Who creates the fruit of the vine

Bread: ha-mo-TZI le-khem min ha-AR-etz, Who causes wheat to grow

Fruit: bo-RAY pri ha-ETZ, Who causes fruit to grow

New fruit of the season: sheh-heh-khe-YA-nu, ve-ki-ye-MA-nu, ve-hig-i-YA-nu la-z'MON ha-ZEH, Who kept us in life and allowed us to reach this season.

Vegetable: bo-RAY pri ha-ah-da-MAH, Who creates the fruit of the earth

After a meal people sing praises to God:

Let us praise God, Lord and King over all,
God's great love and kindness
cover all living things.
God has given food for the whole world,
May we never be in want of any food.
God has provided enough for all.
Let us give thanks to God's great name.

Psalms

Over the holidays, many psalms that sing the praises of God are recited. Here are a few of them.

From Psalm 16
God is at my side, I shall not be moved.
Therefore does my heart exult and my soul rejoice.

From Psalm 27
The Lord is my light and my salvation,
whom shall I fear?
The Lord is the stronghold of my life;
of whom shall I be afraid?

From Psalm 90
Before the mountains were born, or earth
and universe created,
from eternity to eternity, You are God.

ROSH HASHANAH EVE

This is a busy day. What used to be the New Moon Festival is now Rosh HaShanah. The holiday starts in the evening, at nightfall. The Jewish day begins not after midnight, but with the coming of darkness. Why? The Bible, in the story about how God made the first day, says, *There was evening and there was morning*. Since evening was mentioned first, the ancient rabbis used the Bible verse to shape the Jewish day.

On Rosh HaShanah Eve, people are busy preparing for the evening meal and the home celebration. But first they take care of some religious obligations. By custom, and by religious law, they do what they can to clothe the naked and feed the hungry. They bring money or food and clothing to people in need. They visit friends and relatives who are confined to their homes or hospitals and bring presents of food or small gifts. They visit old people who have no families.

"Release of Vows" Ceremony

In the morning or during the day, Orthodox men take part in a "release of vows" ceremony at the synagogue. As the men of Jerusalem did two thousand years ago, these men gather before a "court" of three learned men. Each man participating in the ceremony stands and tells the "judges" of the vows to God he has been unable to keep over the year. The "judges" consider his reasons and pardon the man. Then the next man comes up to seek pardon. The "judges" have no real power. The ceremony is more an exercise in moral kindness, where a "court" of men listen to confessions of weakness from other men like themselves.

In some places, this ceremony is performed not on this day but on the day before Yom Kippur.

It is the custom of some Orthodox men also to take part in a *mikveh* — a ritual bath — on Rosh HaShanah Eve. They first shower or bathe to cleanse their bodies in the usual way. Then they immerse themselves in a ritual bath, to cleanse themselves spiritually.

The Home Celebration

The holiday begins at home, with the evening meal. First people say blessings over the lighted candles and over the wine. Then everyone — it is the custom to invite guests — sits down to share the banquet together.

Ideas that began long ago as superstitions remain today as customs. People used to say that what happens on Rosh HaShanah Eve sets the tone for the kind of thing that will happen the rest of the year. This thought still animates all holiday customs.

People hope for a sweet year, so they eat honey. *Hallah,* the traditional Sabbath loaf, is usually braided. But the hallah served on Rosh HaShanah has a different shape. People hope for a smooth, even year, so they serve a round hallah on the holiday.

Everyone dips a piece of hallah or apple into the honey, and says the blessing:

> Ye-HI ra-TZON mi-le-fa-NE-kha,
> A-dow-NAI E-lo-HAY-nu v'El-o-HAY a-vo-TAY-nu,
> Sheh-te-kha-DESH a-LAY-nu
> Sha-NA tow-VA u-me-tu-KA.
>
> > May it be Your will, O God, and God of our ancestors, to renew us for a good and sweet year.

The main meal varies. An Ashkenazi family might serve roast chicken and potatoes. An American Jewish family might serve roast beef. Moroccan Jews might serve stewed chicken, and Turkish Jews chicken with rice. Syrian Jews prefer chicken with noodles. Italian Jews serve an elaborate meal of chicken with parsley and pistachio nuts, anchovies in oil, and other dishes.

Symbolic meanings are reflected in the side or extra dishes. A ladder on the hallah baked of the same bread dough, expresses the wish that the family's prayers might ascend to heaven. Dough baked in the shape of a bird represents the same wish. It also stands for the words of the Prophet Isaiah: *As birds protect their young, so will God protect Jerusalem.* A hallah loaf might be topped with a baked, or plastic, crown, signifying the kingship of God. A separate loaf in the shape of a wing likens the goodness of the people around the table to the goodness of angels.

To underscore the wish for a sweet year, Ashkenazim serve *mehren tzimmes,* a carrot pudding with raisins or prunes. Sephardim serve sugared pomegranate seeds. The Jews of India serve puris, sweet wheat cakes with

coconut. Italian Jews serve a delicious pastry called *sfratti* — "eviction sticks." It is a honey-and-nut dessert baked in the shape of a stick once used by landlords and enemies of the Jews to prod people to leave a building or community. All sweet dishes are served to call forth a sweet year.

What are the things that make for a sweet year? Health, luck, wisdom, and prosperity. These blessings are also called forth by serving other symbolic foods.

Food from the new crop of the season is considered good luck. Therefore grapes, figs, and whatever is being harvested at the time are served.

Sephardim consider foods that grow quickly to be symbols of prosperity. They will therefore prepare dishes with pumpkin, dates, fenugreek, leeks, and beets.

To gain wisdom, Syrian Jews serve blackeyed peas, to help them see better, calf tongue, to help them speak better, and calf brains, to help them think better.

Afghan Jews slaughter a sheep and distribute the parts to the poor, keeping the head for themselves. The head is the symbol of rescue, as it stands for the ram that was sacrificed in place of Isaac.

Fish, because they are numerous, are used as a symbol of fertility and prosperity. And because their eyes are always open, and they see everything, they stand for knowledge. On Rosh HaShanah, the head of the fish is placed before the head of the family. And he or she says, on behalf of all those at the table, "May it be your will that we be like the head (leaders) and not like the tail (followers)."

An Iraqi Jewish family, however, will serve no fish at this time. The Hebrew word for fish is *dag*. The word for worry is *da'agah*. The words are similar. Iraqi Jews are afraid of confusion and take no chances.

A pomegranate is said to have 613 seeds. The number corresponds to the number of commandments, or kinds of good deeds, that Jews as a society must perform. A pomegranate on the holiday table announces to the heavenly court that as many seeds as there are, that's how many good deeds have been performed over the year.

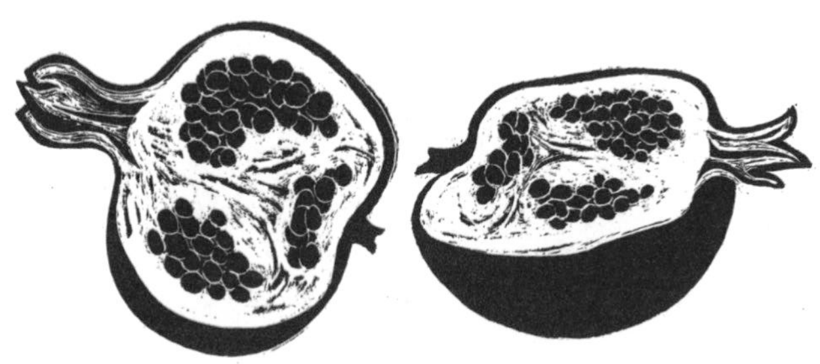

When the feast and fun and merriment are over, everyone goes to the synagogue. Tonight the gates of heaven are opened. The heavenly court convenes, and the three big books stand open. People's names appear in the Book of Judgment. They hope to lead exemplary lives over the next nine days so that their names will be transferred to the Book of Life. Everything they say and do from now on reflects this wish. In the synagogue, they sing praises to God, Master and Judge of all the world. They admit their guilt and plead for forgiveness, saying, *Our Father, our King, hear our voice. Our Father, our King, we have sinned against You. Our Father, our King, have mercy and answer us, for our own powers are limited.* After the evening service, everyone exchanges New Year greetings. "May you be inscribed and sealed in the Book of Life," they say, and wish each other a good, sweet year.

ROSH HASHANAH

And the first day of the seventh month shall be to you a festival of horn blowing. Leviticus 23:24

It is the big day, the day of horn blowing, the day of judgment, the birthday of the world. People are at the synagogue for morning prayers. They declare their pleasure at being in the presence of God, saying, *Through Your great kindness, O God, I come into Your house and reverently pray to You. O Lord, I love Your house, and the place where Your glory dwells. Here will I worship You, O my Maker.*

The Horn Blowing

Two men, or women in a liberal synagogue, mount the platform at the front of the synagogue. One takes up the ram's horn and faces the Holy Ark. There, the Torah, the Bible in scroll form, is kept. While the second person reads from a book and calls out the notes, *"Tekiah!"* (one long note), *"Shevarim!"* (three short notes), *"Teruah!"* (nine shorter notes), the horn blower gives the appropriate blast. The people are stirred by the meanings evoked by the blasts. In the course of the morning, 100 blasts will be sounded in most Orthodox synagogues.

The famous Unetanneh Tokef prayer is recited. Everyone stands. The worshipers cover their heads with the prayer shawls they wear. All proclaim the holiness of this day with the awesome words:

> On Rosh HaShanah it is written,
> on Yom Kippur it is sealed:
> How many shall pass away,
> and how many shall be born,
> who shall live and who shall die,
> who shall complete their years and who shall not,
> who shall die by fire and who by water,
> who by sword and who by wild beast,
> who by famine and who by thirst,
> who by earthquake and who by pestilence,
> who by strangling and who by stoning,
> who shall be at rest and who shall wander,
> who shall be serene and who shall be disturbed,
> who shall be at ease and who shall be afflicted,
> who shall be poor and who shall be rich,
> who shall be humbled and who shall be exalted.

The poem speaks of harsh judgments. But its final words offer hope. It ends:

> But repentance, prayer and deeds of mercy can cancel a severe judgment.

Tashlich — Casting Away

People go home for a holiday lunch. In the afternoon, they prepare for Tashlich. They put bread crumbs, which serve as symbolic sins, in a paper bag or in their pockets. And they go to a river or lake where they cast their "sins" into the water.

Before World War II, the Hasidim of Poland used to prepare a small bundle of straw as their symbolic sins. They marched to the river in a group, with lighted candles. They prayed until sunset. Then they set fire to the bundle and set it on the river. Their "sins," consumed by fire, floated away in the growing darkness.

Moroccan Jews practice Tashlich not on this day but on Yom Kippur. Marranos, the secret Jews of Portugal, practiced the ceremony on the last day of Passover. This might have come about from their need to disguise or hide their actions, so as not to be discovered by the authorities.

Today, most Jews empty their pockets, or paper bags, over the water and either read to themselves or have someone read aloud from Psalm 33:

Our soul has waited for the Lord;
God is our help and our shield.
For in God does our heart rejoice,
Because we have trusted in God's holy name.
Let Your mercy, O Lord, be upon us.

Or from Psalm 130:

Out of the depths have I called to You, O Lord.
Lord, hearken to my voice;
Let Your ears be attentive
 to the voice of my pleas.

Or from the last chapter of the Book of Micah, the prophet:

[Speaking to God]
They shall come with fear unto the Lord our God
 And shall be afraid because of You.
Who can compare to You?
Only You can forgive our sins and
 overlook the wrongdoings of the remnant of Your people.
You do not remain angry,
 but delight in mercy,
[Speaking now to the people]
Only He can forgive sin
 and overlook the wrongs of the remnant of His people,
 He does not remain angry
 but delights in mercy.
He will again have compassion upon us;
 He will subdue your wrong acts,
 and cast all your sins into the depths of the sea.

Today, new versions of the Tashlich ceremony are arising. One was created by people who live inland and do not have access to water. They sit in a circle on the floor, a bowl of water before each person. Each one has written on a slip of paper in water-soluble ink some sin or habit he or she would like to get rid of. They read aloud from favorite psalms or poems they have written for the occasion. Then they read the words of Micah, toss the slips of paper into the bowl, and watch the water wash away their sins.

The second day of Rosh HaShanah is often a repetition of the first day, sometimes of just parts of it. Although people return to school and work afterward, they are aware of the themes of repentance and forgiveness as they wait for Yom Kippur to arrive.

YOM KIPPUR EVE

> On the tenth day of the month shall you afflict your souls and you shall do no manner of work. For on this day atonement shall be made for you, to cleanse you of all your sins and you shall be clean before the Lord. Leviticus 16:29–30

The Kapparot ceremony is performed today. As in olden times, many Orthodox Jews still use chickens. Most Jews who practice this ancient ceremony transfer their sins to money and donate the money to charity. Iranian Jews send flowers to relatives and friends.

In all homes, people eat a festive meal in the evening. It will be the last meal for twenty-five hours. For the many people who fast, no food or drink is taken in that time. Girls from the age of twelve and boys from thirteen (girls are thought to mature earlier) are expected to fast. But health and life are the first considerations. And those who cannot fast need not do so.

Clothing

As in ancient times, the color white dominates the holiday. In homes where people fast, they put a white cloth over the table and books of scripture over it, to show that they will take their nourishment not in food but in prayer. And many men and women wear white, the color of purity, or beige. Throughout the year people wear leather shoes. To enhance the specialness of this day, and its mood, they wear cotton shoes or slippers.

Children's Blessing

Before leaving for the synagogue, many parents bless their children. They place their hands on the head of a child and recite the ancient priestly blessing: *May God bless you and protect you, may God shine His countenance upon you and be gracious to you, may God look kindly upon*

you and grant you peace. Some parents use another blessing or make up their own.

May God make you like Sarah, Rebekah, Rachel and Leah
May God make you like Ephraim and Manasseh . . .

Candle Lighting

The family lights holiday candles and blesses them. Today, they light other candles as well. It is the day to remember those who have died, and they light "soul" candles, in their memory. The black Jews of Ethiopia, have another ceremony for remembering the dead. They put grains of millet on stones outside the synagogue and let birds carry away the food, symbolically feeding the dead.

Although it is Yom Kippur, and a final judgment is about to be made, people leave the house in a good mood. They are not afraid. For they have asked forgiveness of others, and received it. They have granted forgiveness. They have done good deeds. They have asked God for forgiveness and promised themselves to strive for a better character. They are in a good mood because they believe God to be merciful and they expect to be forgiven.

In many synagogues, people also light "soul" candles as they enter. Sometimes there is a separate synagogue in the same building for the children. But in most places, the family sits together.

Not only do people wear white, the synagogue itself is draped in white. White curtains cover the Holy Ark where the Torah scrolls are kept. The inscription on the curtain supports the confidence of the people that they will be forgiven. It quotes the prophet Isaiah: *Though your sins be as scarlet, they shall be white as snow.*

Worshipers wear white prayer shawls around their shoulders. The rabbi, or prayer leader, wears a white robe over his or her suit. In such a robe are Jewish people buried when they die. It is a shroud. The shroud is worn to remind people of their place in the universe: They may plan, but God makes the final decision. They are mortal and must die one day; but God lives forever. The white robe, a *kittel,* may originally have been worn to imitate the white robe of the ancient high priest in Jerusalem. The tragedies that beset the Jews in the centuries of their exile may have added the shroud meaning.

The prayer leader often wears no shoes, just white stockings. This custom also comes from the Bible. In the Book of Exodus, Moses one day saw a burning bush when he was out with his flock. He heard his name called. The voice seemed to come from the bush, and he approached it. As he did so, the voice of God said, *Put off your shoes from off your feet for the place whereon you stand is holy.*

The Torah Scrolls

Those standing on the platform face the Ark. As someone draws aside the curtains to show the Torah scrolls covered in white, the cantor, the liturgical singer, sings: *Or za-RUA la-tza-DIK u-le-yish-RAY lev sim-KHA* — Light will shine on the righteous and joy shall be their reward. Each one takes another scroll from the Ark. Then, marching together, they parade around the synagogue. This gives everyone an opportunity to "hand" kiss or "book" kiss the passing Torah. People touch their fingertips or book to a Torah, then bring book or fingertips to their lips in a kiss. All scrolls but two are returned to the Ark.

Kol Nidre — All Vows

Two people stand on the platform on either side of the cantor. Each of the two holds a Torah scroll. The three together represent a religious court. They have no real power but are only symbolic judges.

In a very few places the Kol Nidre is not said. Instead, the congregation may recite Psalms 103 or 113, which used to be recited in Jerusalem before the Temple was destroyed in 70 C.E. But in most places the Kol Nidre is chanted. And even people who do not go to the synagogue on other occasions come at this time to hear this haunting chant.

As was done in the days of the Spanish Inquisition some four hundred years ago, the cantor declares it lawful to pray with sinners this night. And he chants three times in a mixture of Aramaic and Hebrew, the words of the Kol Nidre:

> All vows and oaths, all promises and obligations, all renunciations and responses, that we have made from last Yom Kippur to this one (or from this Yom Kippur to the next — or both) we cancel. May we be free of them all, may we be released from them all, may they all be null and void, may they be of no effect. May these vows not be vows, may these oaths not be oaths, may these responses not be responses.

In the thirteenth century an unknown musician composed a soulful melody for the chant, and it is this stirring, moving melody rather than the words which has captured the hearts of the people.

People then sing praises to God, thank God, confess their wrongs, and pray for forgiveness.

YOM KIPPUR

Over the course of the day, the long and short confessions are recited several times. People stand together, and as they confess aloud, they tap their chests lightly with a fist as they give voice to each sin. Following the recital they say, *O God of forgiveness, forgive us, pardon us, grant us atonement.*

Torah Readings

On the reading table a Torah scroll is rolled open to the Book of Leviticus. A man lifts the scroll high above his head by taking a roller in each hand. Holding it aloft, with the writing facing the congregation, he, along with others, sings out, *This is the Torah given by Moses to the children of Israel at the command of the Lord.*

Jonah

The Bible story of Jonah is read aloud. This tells how God instructed Jonah to go to the city of Nineveh, the capital of Assyria, and warn the Gentiles to give up their evil ways or they and their city would be destroyed. Jonah did not want to obey God. He thought the people of Nineveh were evil and deserved to be punished, that they should not be given an opportunity to repent. Trying to escape from God, Jonah went down to the port at Jaffa and boarded a ship for Tarshish. But he could not escape God, not by ship and not in the whale's belly. He ended up in Nineveh, where he proclaimed God's message: *If you continue in your wicked ways, Nineveh will be destroyed in forty days.*

Frightened, the king ordered the Assyrians to atone for their sins by fasting. God forgave them. This angered Jonah. God chided Jonah, saying, *Should I not have pity on the great city of Nineveh in which there are more than 120,000 human beings and also much cattle?*

The story is read for several reasons. It shows the power of atonement and says there is no escape from God. It says all people are entitled to God's mercy and to the mercy of other human beings.

The Temple Service Is Remembered

A description of the Temple service of old is read aloud. Following the custom of the ancient high priest in Jerusalem, the modern prayer leader lowers himself to the ground upon the mention of God's name. In some places, the entire congregation prostrates itself.

Neilah — Closing

In ancient times, this ceremony referred to the closing of the Temple gates. Today, it refers to the heavenly gates. They are about to close. The heavenly court is about to disband. The heavenly books are about to be sealed. All rise and repeat the confession, which begins, *Our Father, our King, we have sinned before You. Our Father, our King, we have no king but You.*

The ceremony is ended with clear echoes from the past. The last words spoken by the people are words that were first spoken by Moses: *Hear O Israel, the Lord is our God, the Lord is one.* They then repeat the words of the ancient Jews of Jerusalem, *Blessed be His name, Whose glorious kingdom is forever and ever,* then the words of the Prophet Elijah, *The Lord, He is God.*

Before Israel became a state, people used to end with the spoken wish, *Le-sha-NA ha-ba-AH be-yir-U-sha-LA-yim* — Next year in Jerusalem. That wish has come true. Jews are once more living in Jerusalem. People today say instead, *Le-sha-NA ha-ba-AH be-yir-U-sha-LA-yim ha-shlay-MAH* — Next year in a rebuilt Jerusalem.

Everyone leaves the synagogue in a good mood. They do the bidding of an ancient poet who said,

> Go your way, eat your bread with joy,
> and drink your wine with a merry heart;
> for God has accepted your pleas.

Orthodox Jews this same night begin building a *sukkah* — a booth — to show their eagerness to celebrate Sukkot, the harvest festival, due in four days.

THE HOLIDAYS DURING THE HOLOCAUST

World War II started in 1939, when Adolf Hitler's Nazi armies marched across Europe. World conquest was their first aim. Their second aim was genocide. They sought to rid Europe, then the world, of Jews.

The Nazis, in their scheme of conquest, had a special program for Jews. They herded them into ghettos, to live under guard and curfew. They used them as slave labor to work in concentration camps making products for the German war machine. When the Jews were no longer able to work, they were sent to extermination camps to be gassed to death. In the war years, six million Jews were killed — men, women, and children.

Some Jews lived to tell their stories. Some were killed but left behind diaries that were later found. Michael Zylberberg was a high school teacher in the Warsaw Ghetto, in Poland. His diary notations on the holidays show the deteriorating condition of the Jews during the war years.

Yom Kippur, 1939. Germany occupied Warsaw, seized Jewish property, forced Jews to wear a yellow star on their clothing, and herded them all into the ghetto area. As German bombs fell on the city, Jews gathered in each other's homes to pray.

Rosh HaShanah, 1940. The Germans built a wall nearly ten feet high and eleven miles long around the ghetto to seal the Jews in. Five hundred Jews died daily of hunger, dysentery, and typhus.

Yom Kippur, 1941. Zylberberg and Dr. Korczak, their teacher, organized prayer services for 150 Jewish orphans. All but Zylberberg were dead by the end of the year.

Elsewhere in the ghetto during the holidays, according to one account, Nazi guards patrolled the streets while flowers were thrown over the wall. A card said the flowers were a greeting to the Jews for the New Year from the Christian workers of the Wola factories.

Yom Kippur, 1942. The Germans opened a new death camp, in Treblinka, in Poland. The day before Yom Kippur Eve they searched the ghetto for "nonworking elements." Children who were deemed old enough to work were torn away from their parents. Sick people,

regarded as useless, were shot on the spot. During lunch the Jews placed a guard at the door so they could say the prayer for the dead. Out of a total ghetto population of 400,000, only 60,000 were left. The others died of disease or starvation, or were gassed.

Yom Kippur, 1943. The ghetto Jews revolted against the Nazis. Although they fought heroically with handmade weapons, they had no chance against the German tanks. Except for a few Jews who managed to escape, all were destroyed. Zylberberg hid in a church on Yom Kippur, the safest place for a Jew on the run.

Denmark was the scene of a historic event that same year. Earlier, in 1940, when Germany invaded Denmark, the Germans ordered Danish Jews to wear a yellow Jewish star as a mark of identification. King Chris-

tian X, resenting the order on behalf of his subjects, wore the star himself, as did other Danes. But on Rosh HaShanah Eve in 1943, the Jews received a shock when they gathered at the synagogue for prayer. Their rabbi, Marcus Melchior, said, "There will be no service this morning." He had learned the Germans were planning to arrest and transport all Jews the following morning to a concentration camp. The Jews sat in stunned silence. The rabbi urgently sent them home to pack and phone all their Jewish friends. That night, 7,000 Danish Jews were hidden in the homes of Danish Christians, or in hospitals disguised as doctors, nurses, and patients. When the Germans came to Jewish homes the next day with their lists of Jewish names, they found the homes empty. The night before, under cover of darkness, Jews began to be transported in small fishing boats to the safety of neutral Sweden.

Another country that saved its Jews was Bulgaria. Although allied to Germany, King Boris refused to cooperate with the Nazis' order to round up the Jews.

THE HOLIDAYS DURING ISRAEL'S WARS

In 70 C.E., Rome destroyed the temple that had been standing for some one thousand years, leveled Jerusalem, and drove the Jews from the city. That year, the Jews celebrated their last Yom Kippur in Jerusalem. All that remained of Solomon's Temple was a section of the wall that had surrounded the Temple. The wall became known as the Western Wall and became a shrine for Jews through the ages.

In 1930, Israel, which was called Palestine before World War II, was controlled by the British. A Jewish underground rose up to drive the British from the land, so that the Jews might govern themselves in their own land. The British permitted Jews to pray before the Western Wall but not to blow the shofar. But in 1930, Moshe Segal of the Irgun, the Jewish underground, was arrested. He defied British orders and blew the shofar on

Yom Kippur, to end the fast. Chief Rabbi Abraham Kook called the British secretary asking for the release of Segal. Rabbi Kook said, "I have fasted all day but I will not eat until you free the man who blew the shofar."

"He violated a government order," the secretary said.

"He fulfilled a religious commandment," the rabbi said.

In 1948, after World War II, Israel again became a Jewish state, by decree of the United Nations. In protest, neighboring Arab states made war against Israel. Israel won its independence in that war but lost to Jordan that part of Jerusalem called the Old City, where the Western Wall is located. Jordan made it illegal for Jews to set foot near the wall.

In June 1967, the Arab nations again attacked Israel. And in what has come to be called the Six-Day War, Israel recaptured the Old City. For the first time in two thousand years, Jerusalem was again under the control of Jews. That fall, on Yom Kippur, Prime Minister Menachem Begin sent Moshe Segal to blow the shofar legally and openly at the Wall in a Jewish Jerusalem.

In 1973, Yom Kippur fell on October 6. That day, Syria and Egypt invaded Israel in a surprise attack. Egypt came across the Suez Canal. The Israeli soldiers stationed there were startled by the oncoming tanks and took out their Torah scroll to pray. As shells rained down on them, they fought back with the only weapons at their command, rifles. Even so, they managed to hold back hundreds of Egyptians for a week. When they were captured, the Egyptians asked to see the Israelis' secret weapon. They could produce none. Hilel Unsdorfer, one of the Israelis, later said their secret weapon could only have been the Torah, for that was all they had. The Israelis took the Torah with them when they were taken to Egypt as prisoners. "It watched over us while we were fighting," Unsdorfer said. "We felt it should stay with us and continue to guard us."

And so the four-thousand-year-old cycle of the Jewish year continues, season after season, century after century. Today, in Jerusalem, a soft siren is sounded in the evening. It signals the start of Yom Kippur. Within seconds, the streets fill with people dressed in white, holding prayer books. They are headed for the synagogue. They pause to embrace friends and neighbors and say *Hatimah Tovah!* — "may you be well-inscribed" — and continue on their way. In Jewish communities all around the world people joyfully celebrate their cherished holidays, remembering their past, and praying for a future of peace.

GLOSSARY AND PRONUNCIATION GUIDE

There is a Hebrew sound that has no equivalent in English. This sound is sometimes spelled *ch* and sometimes *h*. Neither spelling shows the correct pronunciation. The sound is represented in the following pronunciation guide by *kh* and is made by pretending to clear the throat of a tiny crumb, but more softly.

Adonai (a-do-NAI) God
Aseret Yemay Teshuvah (a-SER-et ye-MAY te-shu-VA) Ten Days of Repentance
Ashkenazim (osh-ken-ah-ZEEM) European Jews
Azazel (ah-zah-ZEL) Evil spirit, or devil
Elohim (el-o-HEEM) God
Hallah (kha-LA) White bread
HaSatan (ha-sa-TAN) Satan
Kol Nidre (kol NEE-dra) Opening prayer, Yom Kippur eve
Mikveh (MIK-veh) Ritual bath
Neilah (ne-il-LA) Closing
Rosh Chodesh (rosh KHO-desh) Head of the Month, or New Month
Rosh HaShanah (rosh ha-sha-NA) Head of the Year, or New Year
Selichot (se-li-KHOT) Forgiveness prayers
Sephardim (s'far-DEEM) Spanish Jews
Shofar (sho-FAR) Ram's horn
Torah (tow-RA) Bible, Law, teaching
Tzom Lavan (tzom la-VAN) White Fast
Tzomah Rabbah (tzo-MA ra-BA) Great Fast
Yomim Nora'im (yo-MEEM no-ra-EEM) Days of Awe

YHWH (yah-WEH) God
Yom HaDin (yom ha-DEEN) Day of Judgment
Yom Harat Olam (yom ha-RAT o-LAM) Day the World Was Created
Yom Kippur (yom ki-PUR) Day of Atonement
Yom Teruah (yom te-ru-AH) Day of Shofar Blowing
Yom Zicharon (yom zi-kha-RONE) Day of Remembrance

OTHER BOOKS ABOUT ROSH HASHANAH AND YOM KIPPUR

Drucker, Malka. *Rosh Hashanah and Yom Kippur: Sweet Beginnings.* New York: Holiday House, 1981. For age 10 up, an explanation of the holiday and how to make symbols and crafts.

Goodman, Philip. *The Rosh Hashanah Anthology.* Philadelphia: Jewish Publication Society of America, 1970. An all-inclusive anthology for age 12 up — history, stories, customs, music, recipes, and more.

———. *The Yom Kippur Anthology.* Philadelphia: Jewish Publication Society of America, 1971. Same as above.

Greenfeld, Howard. *Rosh Hashanah and Yom Kippur.* New York: Holt, Rinehart, & Winston, 1980. A short history of the holidays, handsomely produced.

Saypol, Judyth R., and Madeline Wikler. *My Very Own Rosh Hashanah.* Rockville, MD: Kar Ben, 1978. An inexpensive, well-done paper-covered introduction to the holiday for very young children.

———. *My Very Own Yom Kippur.* Rockville, MD: Kar Ben, 1978. Same as above.

Schauss, Hayyim. *Jewish Festivals: From Their Beginnings to Our Own Day.* New York: UAHC, rev. ed., 1969. A full and lively account of the holiday, ancient and modern, for age 12 up.

INDEX